AF368518

Ode to toni morrison

(and COLLECTED *poems...)*

By

JENNIFER BROWN BANKS

Copyright© 2022 JENNIFER BROWN BANKS

ISBN: 978-81-8253-888-7

First Edition: 2022

Rs. 200/-

Cyberwit.net

HIG 45 Kaushambi Kunj, Kalindipuram

Allahabad - 211011 (U.P.) India

http://www.cyberwit.net

Tel: +(91) 9415091004

E-mail: info@cyberwit.net

No part of this book may be reproduced or transmitted in any form or by any means, electronic, mechanical, photocopying, or otherwise, without the express written consent of JENNIFER BROWN BANKS.

Printed at VICORE.

Dedicated to

The late memory of my mother, (Arabella), that continues to inspire and instruct me.

To my family members and friends, for their love and support.

To members of Poets United to Advance the Arts… for more than words can say.

And to the glory of God, "for the things he has done."

Poetry excites,

Unites,

Takes us

On an endless flight,

To lands unimagined,

And celestial

Heights

OTHER POETRY TITLES BY THE AUTHOR

A PARADOX IN PINK

AMIDST QUIET HOURS

YOU GOT A TAB WITH GOD

UNDER THE INFLUENCE OF LOVE

THE LEATHER PANTS (AND OTHER PROVOCATIVE
PIECES)

SEVEN WIDE

CONTENTS

CHAPTER 1

REFLECTIONS

ON THE OTHER SIDE OF THIS PANDEMIC

On the other side/of this pandemic
There's a message that persists
Perhaps
A divine lesson that exists
Beyond logistics?

Is it a wake up call
For us all?
A curse
For living outside
Of God's laws?

A reminder
To live kinder?
A warning to repent?
 Prelude
Of an apocalyptic event?

The dawning of a new day?

No one can clearly say…

But what I believe
For sure,
If we are to endure
And overcome this,
God must be the "cure"

For this situation
Is truly demanding,
And exceeds our human capacity
For understanding,

So at the end of the day
Let us bow our knees
And humbly pray
This virus away.

ODE TO TONI MORRISON
(1931-2019)

Always thought
That we'd connect
Beyond words
On the page—
In a future time and space,
Perhaps in some
Quaint coffee shop,
With an assortment of herbal teas
And pricey brews,
Or a university lecture
Of fellow intellectuals,
Or a book signing
Of eager readers,

Me
Full of awe and admiration,
Unfulfilled dreams
And endless questions,
Hoping to emulate,

You
Worldly,
Wise,
Strong,
Spirited,
Grounded
Like a mighty oak,
Tall,

Brown,
Statuesque,
Cloaked in black,

Now fate
Has deemed it
Too late
As you close out
Your final chapter,

And your writings
Remain
Etched
In our hearts

A WHITE MAN BEARING GIFTS...

Momma said,
Never talk to strangers,
But he was so nice,
Didn't think twice,

Him,
Forbidden,
Motives
perhaps
Hidden,

Bearing gifts,
Offering up
Compliments,

Sugary,
Dripping
effortlessly,
From his tongue
Like caramel

Obviously,
Keenly aware,
Of my
Sweet tooth

FLESH OF MY FLESH (FOR MY SON)

Flesh of my flesh
More than you know
I wish you
Peace
In a troubled world,
God's grace
And protection
Recollection of my teachings
To guide your direction,

I wish you joy and happiness,
Meaningful moments
Void of anger and stress,
Work that fills your soul
And rock-star success,

Flesh of my flesh
More than you know
I wish you
Simple pleasures,
Friends you treasure
More love
Than you can measure,

Flesh of my flesh
More than you know
I wish you good health
Acceptance of self,
And spiritual wealth

Flesh of my flesh
More than you know
I wish you
Life's best

ODE TO ADAM

Despite
All my worldly independence,
It is from you I draw my strength,

As the creator divinely meant,
Our differences complement,

Your dominant energy
Feeds my femininity,
The yang to my yin,
Always balancing,

Adam,

The stronger vessel,
Your appointed role,
Essential…

Plucked from your rib,
Close to your heart,

The whole
To my part

MURAL, CHICAGO

Like sloppy graffiti,

The ugliness of violence
Keeps "defacing"
The walls of our town—

The scarlet red
Of bloodshed
Too often being found,

Splattered,
Scattered,
"Tagging"
A once beautiful
Mighty image—

Inscribing it with
An indelible ink permanence,

History won't soon forget

SILLY
(CIRCA 2005)

Today,
It seems rather silly,

How yesterday
Thought I couldn't live
Without you
Being part of my
Tomorrows,

And now,
Years later,
I stumble across
Your photo
And struggle
To remember
What the fuss
Was all about

They say hindsight is 20/20...

As I laugh
At just how
Silly
I was back then

SUNDAYS AT MOM'S PLACE

The years have
Softened her
Like butter
Left out
At room temperature,

Her once
Vibrant,
Vivacious
"Take-no-shit"
Personality
Now
Held hostage,

Gradually,
Imprisoned
By the passage of time,

Replaced by
A new identity
I have yet
To know fully,

We must both surrender,
To the latest reality,

These days,
She walks slowly,

Calculating each step
Cautiously,

Often needing me to repeat things
Repeatedly,
Often needing me to repeat things
Due to diminished hearing,

Her mind,
Still sharp,
But, less reliable,

I cook her dinner—
Short ribs,
Candied yams,
Peach cobbler,
A few of her
Favorite things,

We talk,
Laugh,
Reminisce,
Over cherished memories,

I give instructions
On kitchen safety,

As she struggles
To re-learn
Things she once
Taught me

EVEN IN DEATH, WE LIVE

Even in death
We live,
Eternally,
Each mighty limbs
Of a family tree,

Connected intrinsically,
Rooted in rich history
And beautiful memories,

MIGHTY,
You and me,

Beyond geography
Without time boundaries,

Always growing,
With love overflowing,

For generations to come,
Even in death,
We live

7 WIDE

Feet

That deserve to be pampered,

Are pounding the pavement,

Keeping pace with the frantic beat

That has become the symphony of

My life-

Running errands,

Running ragged,

Sometimes

Feeling as if I'm running in place,

Immobilized by fear.

Feet that could speak

Volumes

On places they've been,

Stories

That would make you laugh,

Some that would make you cry,

Feet

Enlightened from the journey.

Feet,

Flat, wide, aching

With toes polished

In shades of tantalizing pink,

Seeking to be Sexy

In clearance-rack pumps

Too tight

Heels too high,

Adding jiggle to my wiggle,

Auditioning to be,

Feet

Worthy of his fetish,

Feet

Ultimately hoping

To be shelved,

By a man who dares

To sweep me off of them

I IS FOR INVISIBLE

Growing up
As kids,
We deemed it
Pretty cool
And super clever
To be invisible,

To navigate
Time and space
Unseen,
Unheard,

To avail other's secrets—
Be a fly
On the proverbial wall
Without human detection
Or detriment,

Little did I know
Years down the road
As a Black woman,
I would be granted
This status
Without aspiration or effort
In society's eyes,
Without
My own
Volition—

Be careful
What you
Wish for

THE LEATHER PANTS

Soft,
And shapely packed
In midnight black,
Stopped you
In your tracks,

Subtle
With great impact,
The kind that
Turns heads back,
Stacked

As I crossed your path,
You smiled,
Impressed
We talked awhile,

Clever,
Leather,
Well put together,

More than a fashion statement,
More like a mission statement,

Purposed to make you wonder,
The feel
Of my thunder…

THE UNSPOKEN

Galvanized by fear
They live in
Gated communities
With perfectly manicured lawns,
Dressed in sapphire green
That wink at us
With flirtatious beauty,

Ironically,
With a welcoming appeal,
Yet guarded
From those of us,
Perceived as outsiders,
Or square peg
In-a-hole different,

Remaining
Exclusive,
Undiluted,
Monolithic,

Boasting
The unspoken,

"No coloreds allowed"

As history reminds us,
Trespassing
Carries
Penalties

RESIDENCY

Despite the crime,
Despite the grit and grime,
Despite the rhetoric
Challenging his citizenship,

Let the records show
For all the nation to know
For future generations,
And history's preservation,
That the 1st Black President lived here,

The home of Home Run Inn Pizza,
Buildings tall enough to kiss God,

Frigid winters,
And hot Jazz spots,
Notorious politicians,
The backdrop of fabulously famous writers,
Oprah's former stomping ground,

Chicago,
More than a "toddlin' town"
It's called home for millions,
Where greatness hangs its hat,
A mecca for movers and shakers,
A great source of pride...

ON OUR WATCH!

Kids are losing their innocence,
Way too early,
While the elderly
Are becoming invisible and irrelevant,

Cops are manufacturing
Their own brand of justice,
"Triggering" fear,
Discrimination continues
To relegate Blacks
To the "rear",

People are living on the street,
Too many have too little to eat,
There's moral decay,
Political disarray,
Imminent doomsday,

On our watch,

How long will we sit back idle-ly,
In apathy,
Do nothing,
And watch,

On "our watch"?

IN THE MOVIES

In the movies,
The guilty is never who you
Expect it to be,

The good guys
Mainly win,
And lost souls
Find redemption,

People live
In pristine homes
With perfect lawns,
And neighbors
Who return things
They borrow,

In the movies,
Love lasts forever,
Prince Charming
Always saves the day,

And sound effects
Alert us
To impending doom
Where we disengage,
Simply by
shutting our eyes,

Problems are solved
With a plot twist,
An inner conflict resolved,
Time travel,
Or superhero,
All in the span
Of two hours…

Quite to the contrary,
Art does not
Imitate life

INNOCENT LIES ARE ALWAYS GUILTY

Innocent lies
Are always guilty,

No one ever tells you
That they victimize
In ways we don't often recognize,

Or can measure,

By creating false realities,
Distorting and contorting
Timelines and histories,

Feeding egos
In their mystery,

And no matter
How they came to be,
That they sometimes dwarf
Our integrity

Innocent lies
Are always
Guilty…

TWO PLACES AT ONE TIME

Sitting here with him,
Thinking about you,
Wondering if you're somewhere
Thinking about me,

Thinking about us,
Wondering what went wrong,

Wondering why
No matter how hard I try,
I can't pretend
He makes me feel
Like you used to

HE STAYED...

After the dance of romance had lost its footing,

Through cold nights
And heated arguments,
Bearing the weight of the baggage,
Left by men who came before him,
Who didn't quite measure up.

He stayed,
Held my hand through fears,
(Real and imagined)-
 And life's turbulent storms,
Tending to things that needed to be tinkered with around the
house,
And other special projects my body had long before learned to
live without.
He stayed.

He stayed,
Long beyond my expectations,
Like a family visitor,
With a sense of entitlement,
And a hard luck story.
He stayed.

Through my doubts,
And his resolve,
 That he could win me over,

Or wear me down,
With enough time and wine.

He stayed …

FOR A FRIEND WITH ALZHEIMER

I don't know how to rescue you
From the deep valleys of desolation
And frustration,
Of foreign landscapes
Of once familiar things,
Misplaced names
And faces—

How do I restore
Your joy?
Give you back your footing,
Your smile,
Or provide the safety net
That you need
But won't most times mention?

I wish that I could make you feel safe, whole
Help you put back the missing pieces
To your life's puzzle,
But for now,
All I can do,

Is love you
Through

I AM THAT FRIEND...

I am that friend
Of which everyone
Can depend,
Come thick or thin,

To Travel to the end,
Keep secrets
To the death bed,
Time and time again…

So how come when,
My back's against the wall,
There aren't many I can call,
To truly reciprocate?

ENCORE

Sitting in my kitchen,
You talk,
I listen,
As the sun serenades us
In the wee hours of the day,

So much to learn,
So much to say,

Getting to know you,
Getting to know me,
Over a bowl of Frosted Flakes,
And some instant coffee,

In the exchange
I come to realize,
How much I desire you,
How much I admire you,

Feeling familiar
Yet new,

How I look forward to…
More minutes,
Hours,
Days,
Weeks,
Years,
Of sharing dreams

And fears,
Laughter
And tears,

Like now,
Like here

LOVER MAN

For the hard to reach things
Around the house,
I be needing you

For your easy laughter
And the way you cause comfort
To my sleep,
I be needing you

For borrowed strength
And joy leant,
This woman
Be needing you

FOR MIKE B

Your essence
Can not be captured
By mere words
Or modern inventions,
In fact,
(There's no App for that)

Words
Seem insufficient
To express
The eloquence you possessed
To reflect
A gentle soul
With a warm spirit
A quiet intellect,

A modern-day hippy,
A throw-back from the sixties,
Wearing a long beard,
Short on fashion cues,
Sporting brillo-like hair,
Without a care,
Punctuality, rare

A man of few words,
Who touched many,
A poet, gifted

A gentleman,
A friend,
Someone who refused
To be a slave
To time,
Or keeping up with the Joneses,
Or imposed societal dictates,

Always smiling,
And now
From Heaven…

FOR STRANGERS WHO LOVE BOOKS

We have never met
And yet are
Intimately connected,

Strangely,
Inextricably
Bonded

By the ecstasy
We share
Whenever words
Meet page

And our hunger
To know,
Explore,
Understand,
Escape,
Relate
Feel,

Is fed

SOLITUDE

In a world full of
Endless chatter
Born of senseless things
That rarely matter,

With Facebook feuds,
And videos
Gone viral,
With staggering views,

I. Seek. Solitude.
Quiet time,
To reflect,
De-stress,
Process,

To renew,
As I choose

CHAPTER 2

LESSONS

THE PROGNOSIS

While watching TV
On the lay
A disturbing commercial
Came my way,

One declaring
Imminent doomsday,
For couch potatoes
Sedentary in their way,

"Sitting is the new smoking"
They reportedly say,

And much to my dismay,
This non-smoker
Is now up to
One pack a day!

PARENTING IS LIKE BAKING A CAKE...

You take the best
Ingredients,
Combine,
Incorporate
With exacting measures,

Carefully
Follow directives,
Add
A heaping helping
Of love,

Mix,
Mold,
Hover over,

Say a silent prayer,
That your
Painstaking efforts
Will ultimately yield
Something
You can be
Proud of,

And hope
It rises

AINT IT SIILLY? REALLY!

Ain't it silly, really?

How families part,
As readily as the Red Sea,
Simply because they disagree,
Over ancient history,

Or money,
Or sibling rivalry,
Or hurtful words
Uttered mistakenly,
Ain't it silly, really?

How we undermine
Bloodlines that God assigns
Selfishly

How narratives sometimes differ
Of the same story,
Ultimately
Causing another nut
To fall off the family tree

Ain't it silly, really?

A LOSING BATTLE

I'm gaining pounds
In leaps and bounds,
My figure now reveals,

A fate I'm sure
I must endure
For rich and fattening meals,

I've tried to negate
This added weight,
For months I did
Deny it,

Then self-control
Became my goal
And I began to diet,

This plight you see
Is new to me,
And so far all I find,

The only thing diminishing
Quite frankly
Is my mind!

THE DADDY DEFICIT

Some poke out their chests
Like peacocks
In stride,
To reflect their pride,
For planting seeds
That populate the earth,
In this, they find worth,

And that's as far as it extends,
The emotional connection ends,
They become like Houdini,
When the real work begins,
Separating the boys from the men,

AND WITH THIS…
Their offspring become statistics,
Get lost in the system,

AND WITH THIS…
Daughters left on their own
Are more prone
To have kids before they're grown,
To seek affection
From the wrong direction,
Young boys never truly become
Men,
For lack of role models to depend,
And absent disciplinarians,

AND WITH THIS
Single mothers
Must do double duty,
And bear the weight
That often becomes too great,

AND WITH THIS…
Corrective measures
 Are met with resistance and hate,
As the destructive cycle continues to perpetuate,
AND WITH THIS
The reality persists..
We all pay
When a daddy deficit exists

4 GEORGE FLOYD

Nobody wins,
When the injustice
We seek to avenge
Is overshadowed
With a victory that's
Shallow,

A war waged
With looting,
Shooting,
Senseless violence
Disorderly protests
And civil unrest,

Nobody wins—

Nobody wins,
When history's former lessons
Go unheeded
And progress impeded—

By ghosts
Of yesteryears,
unresolved fears,
And a
 broken system,
With a pathology
Yet to be
Remedied,

Nobody wins,
 With hatred
And an
"Eye for an eye" mentality,

For the inescapable reality
Is violence
Begets violence
Plain
And simply
For in the end
LOVE. ALWAYS. WINS.

DEADLY DEEDS

Dividing property
Of the deceased
Can sometimes

Divide Families
Divide loyalties

Add to misery
Erase history
Soil memories,

In the end
Burying life
long bonds.

THEY WIN!

When you harbor hate,
Hold a grudge,
Give less than your best,
Fail to see
The beauty of this world,
Become victimized by fear,
Refuse to give benefit of the doubt,
Seek revenge,
Close your heart
To love,
The ghosts
Of your past
Win

SMALL TALK

Of those who speak ill about me,
Let them say what they will,

For the Lord
Knows my heart,
And the depths
That I feel

CHAPTER 3

ETCETERA

4 AMANDA GORMAN

"The Hill We Must Climb"
May not be
Fully ascended
In our lifetime,
(As people of color)
Still we
Continue to
Keep our heads held high,
And our spirits Strong,
In homage to our ancestors,
As we soldier on,

United in our Journey,
Well equipped
For the battle

DEEP PURPLE

(4 the Singer formerly known as Prince)

He left the party early,
Dressed
In purple wings and glitter,
Causing time to stand still,
Like 1999...

Then the music stopped
For all of us,
Leaving hearts
Of purple tears,

Forming
Purple Rain
Purple Rain…

HOW DO WE UNSEE THE INSANITY?

How do we unsee the insanity?
Of
Abuse against the elderly,
Babies having babies,
Celebrities treated
As deities,
Rampant violence,
Ransomed by
Repeated silence,

Disrespect
By those sworn
To serve and protect,
Corrupt politicians,

Rising inflation,
Centuries of discrimination
Decreasing morality,

How do we unsee the insanity?
And more importantly…

When will it end?

IN MEMORY OF ARABELLA

(In loving tribute to my mother)

We were
Debbie Reynolds
And
Carrie Fischer
Kind of close,
A bond
Uncommon
To most—

She was my biggest
Critic,
My most loyal
Fan,
My
Emotional
"Right hand,"

We spoke
Nearly everyday,
Laughing
Over silly
Girl's stuff,
And troubles
Along life's way,

Little did she know
For me

She was the equivalent
Of a
Super hero,
My role model,
Sometimes
My foe,

It still
Remains a mystery,
How she raised 5 kids
And kept her sanity,

Later down the road
Returned to college
Successfully,

To complete
A 4-year degree

Battling health challenges
Bravely,
Intermittently,

She was kind,
But never failed
To speak
 Her mind,

No bigger inspiration
Could I ever find,

In this final chapter,

Through death
And living,

Her legacy
Is the gift
That keeps
On giving…

HAIKU 4 U

(DEDICATED TO MOM)

You are my North Star
Amid life's confusing times
Your teachings remain

TO WRITE POETRY

To write poetry is
To seduce the senses,
Capture the soul,
Stimulate the mind,
Touch the heart,

To write poetry is
To unpack emotions,
Examine,
Illuminate,
Inspire,
Entertain,
Engage,
Connect on paper,
Chronicle personal stories,
Share universal emotions,

To write poetry is
To present the world
Through a broader lens,
Create a paradigm shift,

To know divinity

HANDS

(Dedicated to L.F.)

TO THE MAN
WHOSE HANDS
CHAUFFEUR ME TO WORK
ON BITTER WINTER MORNINGS—

WHOSE STRENGTH
RESCUES JAMMED JELLY JARS
STUBBORN LOCKS,
AND THINGS PERCHED
HIGH
IN HARD TO REACH PLACES

HANDS THAT TINKER,
TOIL,
PAINT,
PRAY,
PROVIDE,
AND OCCASIONALLY PREPARE
FRIDAY NIGHT DINNERS,

HANDS THAT SOOTHE TEARS,
PROVIDE PLEASURE,
UPHOLD,

VERSATILE,
DARK,
LIFE LINES
LIKE A TREE BARK—
HANDS THAT HOLD THIS HEART

NEVAEH

Beautiful little girl,
You are my world,
A source of pride,
You are
Joy personified

TO FUTURE CREATIVE ARTISTS

Read the greats,
Learn,
Modify,
Emulate,

Don't procrastinate—
Immortality awaits!

HOME (MORE THAN BRICKS AND MORTAR)

A fortress
Against the elements,
Ground zero,
For a son
Taking flight too soon,

The Holiday Inn
For folks seeking refuge,
A constant presence
On my "things to do" list,

Quiet,
Clean,
Quaint,

Equity,
In the future,

A sanctuary,
At day's end,

… Much more
Than
Bricks and mortar

SOME MAN IS MISSING ME... (in 2004)

Maybe,
Maybe it's not my place,
But sometimes,
When I look
At myself,
Naked in the mirror,
I give myself a wink
And I think…

Lord,
What a waste

Some man
Is missing me—

It's not about vanity,
Rather the insanity,
As I imagine
The possibilities,
Of what could be,

And think reflectively—
Lord,
What a waste,
Some man
Is missing me

GOSSIP

The elixir
Of fools,
The devil's tool,

So ridiculous
And cruel,

GOSSSSIPPPPP

HONORABLE MENTION

Though you are
No longer
A part of my life,
No longer
Number one,
In my heart,
This poem
Is for you,

For the nights we shared,
Are certainly worthy,
Of an
"HONORABLE MENTION"

THE FINAL CHAPTER

This is it!
The only life
You get,

Live
Without regret,
Forgive and forget,

Be your best yet,

Before the final curtain sets

VALUE

No matter
The presentation,
No matter
How precious the gift,

Not everyone
Is receptive
To
What we have
To offer,

Rather than hanging
Your head
In sorrow,

Consider it their
Loss

www.ingramcontent.com/pod-product-compliance
Lightning Source LLC
LaVergne TN
LVHW041746190726
843493LV00008B/2471